# A Poetic Journey

# Taps;

# The Rhythm of the Heart

Written by

**International Best-Selling Author**

**Award-Winning Poet**

**Rev. Dr. Kevin T. Coughlin Ph.D.**

This book is a work of poetry.


First Printing

electronic editions, and do not participate in or encourage electronic piracy of copyrighted materials. Your support of the author is appreciated.

Printed in the United States of America

Taps; The Rhythm of the Heart is Rev. Dr. Kevin T. Coughlin Ph.D.'s sixth book of poetry. This poetry is an emotional, honest, and raw look at life. The poetry reflects the struggles and hope of day to day life and the journey of the mind and spirit. The author talks about many topics that could impact anyone's life. You will feel the author's anger, love, struggles, hope and so much more through his prolific poetry. Although, there are several poems involving "man's best friend," the book is about the memories we create, the emotions we feel, and the unbearable things and situations that we overcome during our time on this earth. The author wants to honor life and the beauty and struggles during a lifetime.

PLEASE VISIT www.theaddiction.expert for other books written and published by Rev. Dr. Kevin T. Coughlin Ph.D., there you can join his mailing lists for advanced notice on his next books, trainings, and live events.

Disclaimer: In this book, the author shares his experience, strength, and hope with readers, this should not be considered advice. All information in this book is for informational and educational purposes, not medical or psychiatric advice or to prescribe the use of any technique as a form of treatment for medical or psychiatric problems without the advice of a physician, psychiatrist or appropriate licensed professional either directly or indirectly. In the event you use any of the information in this book for yourself, neither the authors nor the publisher accepts responsibility for your actions. The poetry is born of the poet's imagination and does not represent any person living or dead, any similarities are purely coincidence. Please be advised there is some raw adult language used in this book.

## Dedication



This book is dedicated to my Brother, Warren J. Coughlin Jr., close friends and family know him as "Buzz!" My Brother is three years my senior; although, he has always been very young at heart. He is an amazing carpenter and can build just about anything! Buzz has a wife and two sons. My Brother is very ill right now, with malignant pancreatic cancer, but he is not alone! We are all with him and praying for a full recovery for him! We expect miracles in our family! This one's for you Brother, I love you! – Kev.

# Table of Contents

# Shadowland



Dark tides

and

dark times

reflect shadows

in your

bright eyes.

The honest,

the loyal,

the true!

Then the forecast

explodes into

the darkness

that I know as truth!

Still hoping

to be

rescued

from my

Shadowland…

# Jamboree!



Shiny white teeth,

all perfectly strung in a

row,

below

bright eyes filled with light

and life.

Exciting words and promises

entertained the thrill seeker;

now sentenced to life

within the confines

of an old mind.

Mental masturbation

that could bore

a nun playing an organ

at the girl-scout's jamboree!

At night those perfect teeth

wait in a glass

on the nightstand,

next to the thick

eyeglasses

that light up

her wrinkled, old face.

The worn recording of a Sermon

is about to start once again:

"In *the beginning* God created the heavens and the earth…

Now the earth was formless and empty,

darkness was over the surface of the…"

The old women faded,

her eyes shut the world

off,

first came darkness,

then emptiness and nothingness,

as her journey

began…

Cradled in his father's arms,
an illustrious warrior:
admired for achievements,
and noble qualities.

His courage,
the object of admiration.
Sharing dreams and memories,
a student and a teacher:

A father and a son.

© 2016 Rev. Dr. K. T. Coughlin Ph.D.

## Abuse and the Abuser



Abuse comes in many forms:

sadly, too many souls

are touched

by the words,

the behaviors,

and the violence.

Cowards who thrive

on control

targeting

the weak,

the old,

the young,

and infirmed.

Bullies who should be hung

by their fingernails

in a public square,

and stoned to death!

Power

belongs in the hands of

kindness and love.

To define abuse:

to live with

a monster,

where you are trapped,

drowning in hopelessness;

searching for a key

that will let you out

of the room

with no doors.

Remembering

freedom,

resenting the moment.

Losing self with each day,

until your voice

goes silent,

like the whispers

of the mourners

grieving over

their weakness.


© 2018 Rev. Dr. Kevin T. Coughlin Ph.D.

# Beauty and the Beast



It all seems so long ago,

back when I was a drunken fool!

I sat at the bar in White Plains

New York with friends.

We had been there many times before;

however, on that night something

was very different

as I gazed around the room.

My eyes looked on perfection,

my heart missed a beat when I saw you!

My God you were beautiful…

Right at that moment,

you captured my heart,

forever,

and you didn't even know it!

"Shots" for everyone!"

You were so innocent then,

but that would soon change,

it had to.

I wasn't worthy of your love then.

The funny thing is,

when I see you now

my heart still skips a beat.

What I found out

over the years,

is that real beauty

comes from

within.

Friends forever…


© 2019 Rev. Dr. Kevin T. Coughlin

# Existing



Old bones grinding on each other;

cartilage all worn out and gone.

Clicking and popping

with every movement.

Extreme pain

powerful enough

to stop a train,

to stop a life;

taking away all quality.

Old eyes shed tears,

begging for relief.

"Friends" have all

turned a blind eye

to go live their lives.

Rain and snow

feels like an axe

chopping through

old limbs.

No relief in sight

except

the grave…

# Forever Faithful



America has had many heroes

who fought for our freedom.

The Brave, fierce warriors

that risked all for our nation.

There was a fierce warrior,

who was a hero,

amazing, brave, and true.

A Marine,

deployed to Iraq

from Camp Pendleton.

He saved many American lives,

detecting bombs;

some would say,

he was just a dog.

Oh no my friends!

He was a real

American hero.

I just want to say

Thank You

Sergeant Rex!

I'm sure the other Marines

in Heaven

had one word

to say when you arrived,

"Oorah!"

## On the Road

When I was young

and still handsome,

I had a plan.

Travel the world,

become rich,

fall in love,

and grow old

with my love.

Today,

I am old,

I haven't traveled

the world,

I'm not rich,

and not in love.

I have to ask myself

if I have failed at life?

The answer is written

on the faces

of those souls

who my life has

intersected with

and helped to

change them

forever.


© 2019 Rev. Dr. Kevin T. Coughlin

# Paw Prints in The Snow



Another foot of snow;

everything looks so

white and clean.

My two black

dogs

love the snow;

they run and play

jumping like puppies!

Watching them play

in the snow,

is like watching an old

black and white movie.

One likes to throw

the snow

up from the ground

with her nose.

She usually looks like

she just ate a powdered-sugar donut!

When the two get cold enough,

they come racing

back into the house,

leaving paw prints in the snow

for the rest of my life…

© 2019 Rev. Dr. Kevin T. Coughlin

Don't you love gossipers?

Did you hear about Alice?

Did you see what happened to Nick?

What kind of parents are Susan and Phil going to be,

if they're still drinking so heavily?

Did you see that Donny got arrested?

Excuse Me! Excuse Me!

Fucking mind your own business!

Get a life!

I don't want to hear any more!

I don't want to hear!

I don't want to hear about other people's private stuff!

Why are people so noisy and cruel?

Now take that same energy and help someone,

Yes!

Help a stranger and their family!

Change the world!

Make a difference!

Otherwise,

FUCK OFF!


© 2018 Rev. Dr. Kevin T. Coughlin Ph.D.

Pet



I didn't realize

for the first few years,

that I was a pet.

I belong to two dogs

and they belong to me.

I have become part of a pack;

we are forever family.

No matter what happens,

our hearts and souls

belong to each other.

They take care of me

as much as I

take care of them.

My loyal protectors,

fierce, yet loving.

I knew they were

my pets;

however,

It took me

a long time

to realize that

I was their

pet too.

© 2019 Rev. Dr. Kevin T. Coughlin

# Reality Check



When I turned fifty,

my new life came

with a wheelchair.

When I start to feel

sorry for myself,

I shed tears

for all of the

brave Americans

who gave all

to protect

our freedom

and way of life.

Many of our Nation's heroes

died before age thirty.

What the Hell

do I have to

Complain about!

# Sinners and Saints



I wish I were a better man;

one who could be a hero.

Shame blocks my sunlight;

thoughts of a boy

dreaming dreams,

like old men see visions.

The future is yesterday;

tomorrow is forgiven.


©2015 Rev. Dr. Kevin T. Coughlin Ph.D.

## Spider Ping-Pong



I didn't know that you could have

nightmares while awake,

or that people tend to believe liars.

I sit and wait in darkness

empty belly and crippled legs;

you spin your web,

no one come or cares.

Innocent eyes look up at me

I do my best to feed them

and give them water.

You spin my car's tires

with your lies;

I'm so filed with anger and hatred

there is no need for food tonight.

"My son would never drive drunk!"

Foolish woman, he drinks every day

and drives on most of them!

Spreading poison back and forth

spiders, ping-pong, ping-pong!

Listen to his lies but close your mind to the truth…

"How much is my son's salary?"

I don't know?

What's the going rate for

abusers, drunks, and liars today?

Fools,

ping-pong, ping-pong…


© 2018 Rev. Dr. Kevin T. Coughlin

## Thanksgiving



Another year alone with my two dogs.

My sister called from Connecticut,

she stays in touch as best she can.

Ever since I grew wheels,

I think friends became uncomfortable

around me.

Holidays became like every other day

many years ago.

My life is taking care of my girls;

making sure my loves have food, water,

love, and go outside a few times a day.

I don't see people very often, but that's

okay!

I realize that I'm a pack leader now.

The greatest gift I have ever known is

the love and loyalty of my girls.

Today another turkey's life was saved,

as just another day in our home passed.

# The C Word



A lump, a pain

something not

quite right!

Getting worse

by the day.

To the doctor

for a check-up.

Black blob

on the x-ray.

You already know

the one word

that no one

wants to ever hear

from a doctor's

mouth!

Then waiting

for the results

to see if you

rolled a seven

and crapped

out!

© 2019 Rev. Dr. Kevin T. Coughlin

## The Crippled One



People used to see me

until I needed a wheelchair;

Now they bump into me,

ignore me, pretend that

I don't exist.

Being dependent on others

is like a curse!

I can feel their resentment,

when I ask for help,

they don't understand;

I am a prisoner

in this fucking chair!

Everyone wanted to be around me,

when I could walk and run,

help them with their lives,

but the world is cruel!

I am not invisible;

I am a person!

I am alive!

If you can't respect me

for who I am,

then, you are only

proving that you are

the crippled one!


© 2018 Rev. Dr. Kevin T. Coughlin Ph.D.

# The End of Summer



It was the end of Summer,

you looked so happy

when you visited.

We sat outside;

you brought your little dog

and your husband.

We talked under the stars,

while the pup ran around.

You seemed so hopeful

about the future.

I didn't realize that

I would never see

you again!

Your husband said

you were on life support.

A massive stroke

took your life

in the blink of an

eye…



(In Memory of my friend Barbara)

## The Man from Italy



I'm not sure if you were friend or stranger?

You showed kindness when I was a boy;

I looked up to you then.

You left the country, your wife,

and your three daughters;

when you returned

a sad old man, white hair

and cancer,

you remained afar.

When they told me

that you died today,

I didn't know

what to do or

how to feel?

The boy you once knew

shed a tear

because he did love you

brother!

The man knows you not.

# The Wild



She whispers to me,

so only I can hear;

she looks at me so that

that only I can see her.

Her beauty

comes from deep

within her soul,

far from her ancestors,

yet still I can see the moon

reflecting in her stare.

She is wolf,

she is dog,

she is friend!

I am the alpha:

pack leader,

I hear her

whispers in the wind

and the call of her

ancestors,

the call of the wild

dancing

on the mountains.

We are all

one voice

when we learn

to listen to

the pulse

of love.


© 2019 Rev. Dr. Kevin T. Coughlin

## Wide and Deep



The visiting nurse is coming today

to care for a wound on my leg.

Wide and deep,

It should have had stitches!

It was snowing and I didn't really

have a ride that night

to get proper care.

It's over two weeks later,

still wide and deep!

The nurse is late;

my dogs are crying.

They want to get back in bed,

so do I,

wide and deep

under the covers

with my arms around my pups.

Wide and deep

as I throw each pup

a bone.

They both catch them in their teeth.

Outside the snow blankets the earth,

Wide and deep.

The visiting nurse comes

and says,

"This wound is

Wide and deep!"

I was an Idiot

for not getting stitches!

© 2019 Rev. Dr. Kevin T. Coughlin

# We are Beasts



Two-legged

and four-legged

beasts!

We all want

the same things:

food, love protection,

shelter,

and to protect our families.

We are vicious, loving, ferocious

beasts!

Leave our family alone

or pay the price

of the pack.

Remember

we are beasts!

© 2019 Rev. Dr. Kevin T. Coughlin

# The Needle and the Thread



The tailor shop on the Avenue,

where the needle and thread

made clothes sparkle like new!

Hour after hour and day after day,

the tailor's needle and thread

made a perfect fit for each day.

He mastered his craft

with his needle and thread,

as throughout the small village

the tailor's fame spread.

People came from the town

and from all over the state;

no matter the price, no matter the wait!

They brought the tailor

suits, shirts, trousers, dresses, and skirts:

too big, too small, shorten pants,

and sew buttons on shirts!

After decades of sewing,

many hours each day,

the tailor's hair turned from jet black

to stark grey.

Today the tailor shop is dark;

The old tailor is dead!

There on the shop's table

rests his need and thread.


© 2018 Rev. Dr. Kevin T. Coughlin

# Weeds



To all the missing fathers

who have left their sons and daughters,

see the shadows of their beauty

reflecting on still waters.

From seed, they turn to dust,

fruit fallen from God's vine;

you crushed young hopes and dreams

spilling sacred breads and wine.

You could build a bridge back to life,

yet still you close your gates;

the sun sets on holy waters

in the darkness, the reaper waits…

Time will not show you mercy,

when you become the lost;

you shunned the youth of summer,

now feel the winter's frost!

Spring will bring new flowers,

rewards for your life's deeds;

placed above your graves

like you, they turn to weeds.

© 2017 Rev. Dr. Kevin T. Coughlin Ph.D.

## Taps



It's dusk, the night is quiet,

the people wait in anticipation.

A single trumpet cries

a butterfly's lullaby

now that the day is gone.

The pulse of a life is set free

by the haunting, yet beautiful melody.

The calendar and clock wait for no one,

every soul has their moment to become

a butterfly, soaring to the Heavens.

Every life is a gift, even those with

struggles, trials, and tribulations.

We honor those who we love,

as we wait for our own moment

in time to fly to the butterfly's lullaby.

When our date and time comes,

a new journey will begin…

# Heaven's Playground

There is a place

where the innocent rest

and the wind carries

their beautiful music,

song of songs.

A place where

the trees dance

and the sun always shines,

climbing above the rivers

and the mountains;

a game of "hide and seek"

with the clouds and shadows.

A place where

memories chase the heart,

a gentle touch of the spirit;

"you're it!"

Run, run through the grass;

barefoot still works best.

Find a place to hide,

make sure that someone

will always find you;

God's recreation.

© 2017 Rev. Dr. Kevin T. Coughlin Ph.D.

# Doubt



Chills run down my spine,

as I realize that I am alone!

Not just for today,

alone forever!

I have made mistakes,

loved and laughed,

had successes and victories.

Now with age,

my body failing me,

no one has stayed,

to love me,

to touch me,

to help me,

not even to be a friend.

I even doubted God tonight

for the cruelty I've seen

and have experienced

in this life.

The horrible thing is

that I am trapped!

Alone in a body that

doesn't work,

scared and lonely.

The truth is,

I know better.

I am never alone;

God is always with me!

I have witnessed the miracles.

Now, I just need

to pray for a few!

© 2018 Rev. Dr. Kevin T. Coughlin

## Snowed In



The years go by and I ponder,

where are the friends that I loved and

trusted, shared my life with, and

thought would be there

when winter came?

It's a cold world,

Ice cold…

© 2015 Rev. Dr. K. T. Coughlin Ph.D.

# Youth



Remember that special toy,

the one you begged for,

the one you cherished?

Where is it now?


Remember that first date,

that first kiss,

that first love?

Where are they now?


Remember…


When life seemed so fresh,

the world crisp;

parents were saints,

idols, and Gods.


Remember when you dreamed

dreams and had visions,

excitement and wonder

filled you?


Remember and forgive…

© 2009 Rev. Dr. Kevin T. Coughlin PhD.

# The Garden



Attendant festivities of formalities,
where two hearts are joined.
The ceremony of matrimony,
where the seeds of intimacy and friendship
flower into the commitment of eternity.
A lifetime of sharing,
in trust, thoughts, and dreams.
Moments of sunlight and rain,
forgiving the clouds their darkness,
reflecting the rainbow,
tasting the morning dew,
growing together
in the garden of love.

© 2016 Rev. Dr. Kevin T. Coughlin Ph.D.

The whistling wind of winter
dances while I sleep
beneath this cozy down-comforter.
The warmth of a womb,
until I'm delivered into the new day.
Rising with the sun's light,
longing for the moon and stars.
A creature of the night
seeking love in the darkness,
in the coldness, and in the nothingness
of this lonely place:
this barren womb
where the wind sings...


© 2016 Rev. Dr. Kevin T. Coughlin Ph.D.

# Sweet Love



I know the darkness, the sun, and the moon.
I am the tides that reflect the starlight,
the future, and the past.

I feast on friendship and intimacy,
delighting in the spring of the season
with the purest of heart.

I am sweet nectar that flows in the garden.
Streams of light that reflect the sun's rays,
the colors of the spectrum.

Behold the rainbow and the flower of life,
the melody that sounds in each heart:
I am love, sweet love.

© 2016 Rev. Dr. Kevin T. Coughlin Ph.D.

Watching the sunlight reflecting off the crystal-clear ocean.
Feeling the wind run through my heart and soul;
painting a rainbow with every thought and dream.
Riding the waves of the fountain of youth;
knowing of innocence lost.
Hoping for a journey of peace, love, and freedom.
Touching hearts with visions of truth.
Finding a place and a purpose for being;
dancing to the melody of the moment.
Running wild in the moonlight;
laughing through the rain and thunder.
Holding on to life, and giving to the world,
loving my friend until tomorrow comes.

© 2016 Rev. Dr. Kevin T. Coughlin Ph.D.

# Falling



Lantern o' lantern,
sing to my eyes,
fly me to the midnight hour!
Bewitched, beguiled,
cat scratching, howling.
Take me away now,
hurry before I awaken…

© 2015 Rev. Dr. Kevin T. Coughlin Ph.D.

# Rose



My Rose, my rose,
beautiful fragrance of spring:
cool waters quench you,
warm sunlight bathes you.
Tears of morning dew
in the winter's garden:
pierced through the heart
immune to the thorns.

© 2016 Rev. Dr. Kevin T. Coughlin Ph.D.

## Brothers



A son,

a father,

a friend,

a brother,

your brother!

A man,

a child of God.

Look past the scars,

see his true heart;

share his life

in friendship

in brotherhood,

and in trust.

Don't judge

or gossip;

be his friend,

for you are one

in Christ:

forever brothers…

# Tree



A tree in spring looks vibrant and alive,

much like the young climbers of summer.

In the fall majesty and beauty

tempt the eye for a moment;

deep tans start to fade,

picnicking under falling leaves.

Winter's chill on brittle branches

and bones,

a legacy of constant change;

memories rooted in seasons past.


© 2017 Rev. Dr. Kevin T. Coughlin Ph.D.

# Rev. Dr. Kevin T. Coughlin Ph.D. Publication Credits

KTC Publishing Phase IIC Coaching, LLC Amazon.com
*Dark Tides; Poetic Reflections of Life* 2018

KTC Publishing Phase IIC Coaching, LLC Amazon.com
*My Running Journal Book* 2018

KTC Publishing Phase IIC Coaching, LLC Amazon.com
*My Daily Dog Journal Book; I Love Pit Bulls* 2017

KTC Publishing Phase IIC Coaching, LLC Amazon.com
*The Professional Coach's Assistant; A Coaching Workbook and Guide.* 2017

KTC Publishing Phase IIC Coaching, LLC Amazon.com
*My Anger Log and Journal Book for Men* 2017

KTC Publishing Phase IIC Coaching, LLC Amazon.com
*My Anger Log and Journal Book for Women* 2017

KTC Publishing Phase IIC Coaching, LLC Amazon.com
*My Baby's Journal Book* 2017

KTC Publishing Phase IIC Coaching, LLC Amazon.com
*The Master Coach's Life Coach Training Guide 2017*

KTC Publishing Phase IIC Coaching, LLC Amazon.com
*Call Center Professional and Ethics* 2017

KTC Publishing Phase IIC Coaching, LLC Amazon.com
***The Official Gambling Addiction Recovery Coach's
Workbook*** 2017

KTC Publishing Phase IIC Coaching, LLC Amazon.com
***The Official Gambling Addiction Christian Recovery
Coach's Workbook*** 2017

KTC Publishing Phase IIC Coaching, LLC Amazon.com
***My Daily Pet Journal Book; I Love Cats*** 2017

KTC Publishing Phase IIC Coaching, LLC Amazon.com
***My Daily Pet Journal Book; I Love Dogs*** 2017

KTC Publishing Phase IIC Coaching, LLC Amazon.com
***Christian Coaching; Life Recovery Coaching Workbook
and Journal 2017*** Made the Amazon Top 100 Best-Seller
List

KTC Publishing Phase IIC Coaching, LLC Amazon.com
***Christian Coaching:*** **The Master's Guide to Becoming a
Professional Christian Life and Recovery Coach** 2017
Made the Amazon.com Top 100 Best- Seller list

KTC Publishing Phase IIC Coaching, LLC Amazon.com
***Addiction Professionals AMA/ APA Guide.*** 2017 Made
the Amazon.com Top 100 Best-Seller list

KTC Publishing Phase IIC Coaching, LLC Amazon.com
***My Monthly Journal; A Roadmap for Change.*** 2017
Made the Amazon.com Top 100 Best-Seller list

KTC Publishing Phase IIC Coaching, LLC Amazon.com
***My Daily Food Journal; A Daily Food Action Plan for***

*Success.* 2017 Made the Amazon.com Top 100 Best-Seller list

KTC Publishing Phase IIC Coaching, LLC Amazon.com *My Daily Prayer Journal; A Walk with Jesus.* 2017 Made the Amazon.com Top 100 Best-Seller list

KTC Publishing Phase IIC Coaching, LLC Amazon.com *My Monthly Journal Book; a Roadmap for Success.* 2017 Made the Amazon.com Top 100 Best-Seller list

KTC Publishing Phase IIC Coaching, LLC Amazon.com *My Daily Meditation Book.* 2017 Made the Amazon.com Top 100 Best Seller list

KTC Publishing Phase IIC Coaching, LLC Amazon.com *We Can the Anthology; A Collection of Poetry, A Journey Through Addiction and Recovery* 2017

KTC Publishing Phase IIC Coaching, LLC Amazon.com *Prevention; Teaching Teens to Say No to Drugs.* 2017 Made the Amazon.com Top 100 Best Seller list.

KTC Publishing Phase IIC Coaching, LLC Amazon.com *Relapse Prevention; Long-Term Sobriety.* 2017 Made the Amazon.com Top 100 Best Seller list.

KTC Publishing Phase IIC Coaching, LLC Amazon.com *Thirty Days of Thoughts About the Holidays.* 2016 Made the Amazon.com Top 100 Best Seller list.

KTC Publishing Phase IIC Coaching, LLC Amazon.com *Thirty Days of Thoughts About Christian Recovery and the Holidays.* 2016 Made the Amazon.com Top 100 Best Seller list.

KTC Publishing Phase IIC Coaching, LLC Amazon.com *Recovery & Life Coaching; The Official Workbook for Coaches and Their Clients.* Co-Author Dr. Cali Estes 2016 #1 Best-Seller Amazon.com Top 100 Best-Seller List

KTC Publishing Phase IIC Coaching, LLC Amazon.com *Addictions: What All Parents Need to Know to Survive the Drug Epidemic.* 2016 Made the Amazon.com Top 100 Best Seller list.

KTC Publishing Phase IIC Coaching, LLC Amazon.com *If You Want What We Have; A Journey Through the Twelve Steps of Recovery Workbook and Manual* 2015 Made the Amazon.com Top 100 Best Seller list.

KTC Publishing Phase IIC Coaching, LLC Amazon.com *In the Sunlight of the Spirit* Workbook and Manual 2015

KTC Publishing Phase IIC Coaching, LLC Amazon.com *We Can; A Collection of Poetry, A Journey Through Addiction and Recovery 2016*

KTC Publishing Phase IIC Coaching, LLC Amazon.com *We Can 2; A Collection of Poetry, A Journey Through Addiction and Recovery 2016*

KTC Publishing Phase IIC Coaching, LLC Amazon.com *We Can 3; A Collection of Poetry, A Journey Through Addiction and Recovery 2016*

***Tumbleweeds;*** Feather Books Poetry Series a Book of Poetry Written by Rev. Kevin T. Coughlin Feather Books England May 2002 (In Memory of DeWitt)

Wayne Independent Newspaper Honesdale, PA

News Eagle, Hawley, PA

Reading Eagle, Reading, PA Berks & Beyond

www.addictsrehab.com

My RecoveryRadio.com Host Kent Paul Sept. 11[Th], 2016 Interview

BBS Radio Poetry reading

Blog Talk Radio - Interviews

The Serenity Show - Interview

Passion Diva Radio- Interview

Recovery Starts Here- Interview

www.sacredearthpartners.com - Interview

The Broken Brain (Blog Talk Radio) - Interview

www.eatingdisorderhope.com

Keys to Recovery Newspaper Beth Dewey CEO

www.keystorecovery.com

All 4 Ur Addiction Recovery Referral Resource Guide Jenny Clark Owner

Tripadvisor.com

MindBodyNetwork

Grieving Behind the Badge Peggy Sweeny Founder

www.theaddictsmom.com

In Recovery Magazine

The Sober World Magazine

The Soberworld.com

Shout My Book

Bookgoodies.com

Goodreads

Book Reader Magazine

Awesomegang.com

www.christiancoaches.com

Hardrock Favorites

Metalcorp

SixxAMFansPhotos

NEWS CHANNEL 10 EYEWITNESS NEWS CHANNEL.COM

KHQQ6 ABC NEWS

ABC EYEWITNESS NEWS 8 KLKN-TV

FOX14 NEWS AT 9

Erie News Now

NTV Nebraska.TV ABC

Western Mass News Channels 3 ABC 40 Fox 6

ABC9 KTRE

7 KLTV ABC

Fox 19 Now

KXNEWC Eyewitness News

12 WSFA ABC

ABC 6 News WLNE TV

100.7 KFM BFM

Fox 5 KVVU-TV Local Los Vegas

13 WTHR COM Indians News ABC

Eyewitness News 3 WFSB.COM

Fox 12 Oregon

WDRB.COM

Fox29 WFFX.COM

WETV San Diego

HAWAII News Now

Marketers Media

WALB News 10 ABC

Tristate Update.com 13 News WOWK

AM760

WMBF ABC News

KCEN HD ABC KCENTV.COM

WECT6 ABC News

Eyewitness News3 WFSB.COM

WLOX ABC BOUNCE Eyewitness News

Eyewitness News 8

CBS8.COM

News channel 6 KAUZ

SPROUT News

12 Eyewitness News KFVS

KEYC MANKATO News 12 CBS & FOX LOCAL NEWS

3 WRCB TV ABC COM

KNDO 23 NBC

KNDU 25 NBC

The Aurorean, Encircle Publications 1998 Poetry and Essays

Joel's House Publications 1998-2005 Poetry and Essays

Our Journey 1998-2005 Poetry

The Poetry Explosion, The Pen 1999-2003 Poetry

Apostrophe 1998 Poetry

Nuthouse Twin Rivers Press 1998 Poetry

The National Library of Poetry 1998

Lines N' Rhymes 1998 Poetry

The Poetry Church Feather Books

England. Anthology John Hunt Publications 1999 Poetry

A Tapestry in Time. 1999 Poetry Book 18 Poems

Connecticut Department of Mental Health and Addiction Services

The Webster Times 1999 Poetry

The Angel News 1999 Poetry

The Skater won The Editor's Choice Award September 1999 (Our Journey)

The Blind Man's Rainbow 1999 Poetry

Arnazella 2001 Poetry

Feather Books, The Poetry Church 1998-2002

The American Dissident 2002 Poetry

The Good Shepherd Poetry 2002

Ya ' Sou Magazine Essays and Poetry

Colt. Winner Editor's Choice Award Contest Literally Horses 2002

Goodbye My Friend Read on the Radio Rhyme and Reason UBC Europe & the UK September 2001 Read on the Radio in Europe and the UK as a Tribute to those lost on September 11th bombings. My poem was read over the radio for many days.

Tumbleweed Read on BBC Radio in England 2001

Published by Feather Books

Notified by John Waddington Feather that Tumbleweed had been read on BBC Radio in England on Several Occasions.

Stanwich Congregational Flyer Poetry

University of Scranton Panuska College of Professionals Essay 2002

Scranton University 2002 Poetry

The River Reporter Newspaper 2002 Poetry

Unity Community News 2002 Poetry

The Poetry Corner Angelfire.com Poetry

The Poet's Market 2002 Poetry

The Poetry Church England 2003 Poetry

Cover of Wayne Independent News 2003 Poetry

Nomad's Choir 2003 Poetry

Written a series of 9 course manuals for a coaching recovery curriculum. 2014-2015

www.addictedminds.org 2015-2016 Articles Matthew Steiner

www.soberservices.com 2015 Articles

http://fromaddict2advocate.blogspot 2016 Articles Marilyn Davis

LinkedIn 2014-2016 Articles

Two Drops of Ink S.W. Biddulph 2015- 2016 Poetry/ Articles

The Addict's Mom 2016 Articles Blog

Ghostwriter Articles/ Content2014-2016

KEITV12: The Kingdom Hour- Interview

BlogTalkRadio The Kingdom Hour- Interview

RecoveryView.com

Brooklyn TV Interview

## About the Author

Rev. Dr., Kevin T. Coughlin Ph.D., DCC, DDV, DD, IMAC, NCIP is an International Master Coach, trainer, #1 best-selling author, writer, poet, speaker,  a Diplomate Christian counselor, and therapist, he is Board Certified in Family, Developmental, Alcoholism, Substance Abuse, and Grief Counseling, the Reverend is a NCIP interventionist, a Domestic Violence Advocate, Associate Professor for DCU, a Provincial Superintendent (to be consecrated a Bishop in 2017) and so much more; he is an expert in the field of Addiction and Recovery. He was a Founder and Board Member of a Residential Recovery Facility New Beginning Ministry, Inc. and is President and CEO of Phase IIC Coaching, LLC., The former Program Director for The Addictions Academy, and the former Editor in Chief for Addicted Minds & Associates. The Reverend has over forty-seven years of experience with the AA program. He has been working in the addiction recovery field for almost two decades, has helped thousands of individuals and their families overcome all types of addictions, substance abuse, alcoholism, process addiction, shame and guilt, relationship and communication problems, anger management, inner healing, self-image, interventions and much more. He is a published author and has published thousands of poems and articles published throughout the United States and other Nations, he has been interviewed on numerous radio talk shows, television, published in magazines, newspapers, books, and online publications; he has been featured on ABC, CBS, FOX, NBC, and the BBC in the UK. Rev. Kev is a former State, National & World-Champion Powerlifter, and still holds several records. He loves to write, read, teach, listen to music, and spend time with people and dogs. His parents are his heroes.

# Follow Rev. Kev. on Social Media



https://www.goodreads.com/author/show/14874631.Kevin_Coughlin

About.me Link: https://about.me/ktc1961/

http://ilikeebooks.com/if-you-want-what-we-have/

http://awesomegang.com

www.amazon.com/Rev.-Kevin-TCoughlin/e/B01AF6AAAI/ref=ntt_dp_epwbk_0

http://www.barnesandnoble.com/w/addictions-what-all-parents-need-to-know-to-survive-the-drug-epidemic-rev-dr-kevin-t-coughlin-phd/1124049106?ean=9780997700695

http://www.barnesandnoble.com/w/in-the-sunlight-of-the-spirit-rev-dr-kevin-t-coughlin/1124049139?ean=9780997700671

http://www.barnesandnoble.com/w/if-you-want-what-we-have-rev-dr-kevin-t-coughlin/1124049130?ean=9780997700688

http://mybookplace.net/in-the-sunlight-of-the-spirit-a   Rev. Dr. Kev's Social Media Accounts

Facebook

1. Kevin Coughlin:

https://www.facebook.com/profile.php?id=1000084499556
07
2. My Group, Resources for those suffering from addiction and their families: https://www.facebook.com/groups/resourcesforthosesufferi ngfromaddiction/
3. RevKev The Addiction Expert: https://www.facebook.com/RevKev/?fref=ts


LinkedIn

1. Rev. Dr. Kevin T. Coughlin PhD
https://www.linkedin.com/in/revkevnetwork


My Group: The Recovery Community Family and Friends:

https://plus.google.com/communities/11352122514111281
1207


Pinterest

1. Kevin Coughlin: https://www.pinterest.com/ktc1961/
2. My Group Board: Recovery We Can
https://www.pinterest.com/ktc1961/recovery-we-can/


Tumblr

1. https://www.tumblr.com/blog/revkevsrecoveryworld

Instagram

theaddiction.expert


My Websites:

1. www.revkevsrecoveryworld.com
2. theaddiction.expert

Twitter:

1.  https://twitter.com/AuthorRevKev

Rev. Kev's Goodreads Link:

-spirituality-training-manual-and-workbook-by-kevin-coughlin

Friends of Recovery Readers and Reviewers Book Group on Facebook:
https://www.facebook.com/groups/1667708970205824/

**Thank you for reading my work! If you enjoyed my sixth book of poetry, would you consider reviewing it on Amazon.com?  I would appreciate your help in getting the word out on how helpful this book can be in someone's life.  Thank you so much and God bless you! Phil 4:13 — Rev. Kev.**